God is Nothingness:
Awakening to Absolute Non-being

Andre Halaw

I dedicate this book to one of the greatest sages this world has ever known, Sri Nisargadatta Maharaj. Your words opened my mind and heart to the magnificent reality of the Absolute. Praise be to you and the *Parabrahman* you reveal. With the humblest of intentions, I hope this book honors your teachings.

Special thanks to Ellen Marie Chen for her magnificent book, *In Praise of Nothing: An Exploration of Daoist Fundamental Ontology.* It was an invaluable resource, without which this present work would not have been impossible.

And to Nishida Kitaro, the brilliant founder of the Kyoto School. His insights into Nothingness have helped and challenged me beyond measure.

We start, then, with nothing, pure zero. But this is not the nothing of negation. For 'not' means 'other than', and 'other' is merely a synonym of the ordinal numeral second. As such it implies a first; while the present pure zero is prior to every first. The nothing of negation is the nothing of death, which comes second to, or after, everything. But this pure zero is the nothing of not having been born. There is no individual thing, no compulsion, outward nor inward, no law. It is the germinal nothing, in which the whole universe is involved or foreshadowed. As such, it is absolutely undefined and unlimited possibility—boundless possibility. There is no compulsion and no law. It is boundless freedom.

—Charles S. Peirce

Only a fool or a man would believe that God is masculine.
Fathers don't create anything; mothers do.
—Common wisdom

There is only one thing to be understood,
and that is that you are the formless, timeless unborn.
—Nisargadatta Maharaj

A monk asked Ch'an Master Zhaozhou, "Does a dog have Buddha nature?"
Zhaozhou said, "*Wu* [Nothing]."
—*Wumenguan*

All things are born of being; being is born of nonbeing [Nothing].
—*Tao Te Ching*

2

Preface

This book is about Nothingness, the great Void of the holy sages, not to be confused with the nothing of the ordinary person.

Silence. A blank page or space in a book. A shout. Slapping the table or thumping the floor. These are all expressions of the ineffable truth that is the universal nature of reality. Since there is no way to directly capture the highest truth with language, all we can do is point to it.

And "Nothingness" is the best verbal pointer that I have found.

In the beginning, there was only Nothing.
Now there is only Nothing.
In the end, there will be only Nothing.

There always was, is,
and only ever will be
Nothing.

God is Nothingness
Christ is Nothingness
Buddha is Nothingness
The Tao is Nothingness
Brahman is Nothingness
The Absolute is Nothingness

Nothingness is neither something nor the common nothing;
it is the Great Nothing, the eternal, magnificent, all-encompassing
Nothingness that transcends being,
yet is the ground from which existence itself arises.

In truth, there is only Nothingness,
for nothing else ever was.

Beings suffer because they do
not understand Nothing.
Intoxicated by their senses and minds,
they chase mirages,
construct temples,
conduct empty rituals,
pursue wealth and status,
believing that there is some*thing*
—meaning, purpose, salvation—
to attain.

Fools are slaves to their senses and thoughts,
caught in the snare of form and desire,
unaware that all things
arise from Nothingness,

---

[1] Okay, if you insist on a title for this poem, you can call it "Ode to Nothingness."

abide as Nothingness,
and return to Nothingness.

For nothing has ever happened.

Existence and appearance are flashes of Nothingness
superimposed upon Nothingness.

There are no beings, no worlds,
no minds, no consciousness,
no souls, no events, no time,
no space, no Buddha, no Christ,
no Self, no God.

There is only the not-'that' That—
the Great, Magnificent Void,
the womb of all existence.

NOTHINGNESS.

Bound by neither space nor time,
Nothingness is dimension-less,
time-less, and form-less.

The Void is unborn, unoriginated, unconditioned, and deathless,
neither coming nor going, 'creating' nor destroying, rewarding nor punishing.
It has never set anything in motion nor caused anything to happen.

Ultimately, there is only Nothing,
which is the final and only truth.

Nothingness cannot be seen with eyes,
nor heard with ears,
tasted with the tongue,
smelt with the nose,
felt by the body,
or known by the mind.

Do not look for it with your senses or mind,
for the Void is beyond color, sound,
smell, taste, touch, form, and
thought.

Transcend them and realize that you are truly
Nothing, that in reality
there is only Nothing.

Then you are free to dance and play
on the waves of Nothingness.

Introduction

This may sound like a very strange book for a Buddhist to write. After all, Buddhism is by and large non-theistic, and not very concerned with the priorities of theistic religions, such as creationism, an afterlife (at least an eternal one), or the fulfillment of prophecy. This, paradoxically, makes Buddhists perfect candidates to write about God—because we are not constrained by any theological doctrine whatsoever. Unlike a theologian or theist of any sort, I do not have any sectarian position to defend. This affords me the advantage of an outsider's perspective.

That and I am an atheist. At least I am inasmuch as I do not believe in any traditional, anthropomorphic Creator with human priorities or intelligence. I am, however, aware of the formless reality at the root of all mundane existence. Buddhists call this "Nirvana," "Dharmata," "Tathata," or "Dharmakaya"; *Advaita Vedantins* "Brahman'"; Taoists the "Tao"; and so on.

Astute readers may have noticed that I omitted mentioning God and any theistic religions in the previous example; this is because the term has so many connotations to so many different people that it is difficult to know exactly what people mean when they say, "God."

To a New-Ager it might refer to "everything."

To Wiccans it may mean Goddess or the Mother.

To a Catholic it represents the Holy Trinity.

To an Evangelical Christian…

You get the idea. God is often a mish-mash, blanket term that can refer to anything from the physical cosmos to a higher order or principle governing the universe; it can point to objective matter or a Being who transcends the material world altogether. The word can be very confusing because it encompasses so many varied concepts, expressing everything from an object of deep religious veneration to a meaningless verbal expression (as in, "Oh my God…").

This is why I generally I avoid using the word. In the many Dharma talks I have delivered as a Zen Buddhist teacher, I have uttered "God" on perhaps three or four occasions, and primarily for dramatic effect.

I don't oppose the word on a religious basis, but on a semantic one; for as a high school English teacher, I always encourage my students to use language with exactitude. Whenever I hear people utter the word "God," I wonder what they mean, to which of the myriad definitions they are referring.

So I will be very clear from the start how I will be using the word "God" throughout the book. God is...Nothingness.

Defining Nothingness is my first and last goal, not the relative "nothing" that stands opposite to "something," but *Nothing* with a capital "N." And I assure you that there are worlds of difference between the two, as wide of a gulf as between an atom and an atom bomb.

The Nothing that I refer to has no opposite; it is the nebulous source[2] and true nature of all that exists. The statement "God is Nothingness," is not the same as saying "God does not exist," quite the opposite, in fact.

I am not dismissing God, I am qualifying it as Nothingness.

Realizing and becoming Nothingness is the most important matter in life. It is the Great Truth; the Origin or Source; the undying, unconditioned, unborn, unmanifest Absolute. In Buddhism, we call this Resolving the Great Matter, Reaching Enlightenment, or simply *Nirvana*; in Hinduism, it's known as *Moksha,* Sanskrit for "liberation." Meister Eckhart, the medieval German theologian called it *Gottheit* or "Godhead." In Western theistic terms, people might call this Finding God.

No matter what we name it, it amounts to the same thing: awakening to the transcendent realm of Nothingness that is ever present and always available to us. Thus, it is both transcendent and immanent at the same time.

Not only is God Nothingness, but so is Buddha. Time. The world. And of course you and I; we are all Nothingness, too.

And that's great news.

A note on the text: despite the awkwardness of using "It" as a pronoun for God, I find

---

[2] Though not in any conventional Creationist sense.

it much more appropriate than "He." Employing a gender-laden pronoun would contradict the entire premise of this work. To clarify, when I write the word "God," I do not refer to a being, entity, or Creator with any sort of human qualities, such as intelligence, motive, preferences, etc. Also, throughout the book I have tried to standardize the term "Tao," opting for the Wade-Giles form over the more modern pinyin "Dao" for consistency, and because I think that most readers are more familiar with the classical form, "Tao." In all cases, I have used brackets [ ] to indicate my alterations. Lastly, for stylistic purposes, I occasionally employ "Nothing" in lieu of "Nothingness." For all intents and purposes, I intend them to be semantically identical.

This book might be more aptly entitled, ***Nothingness** is God*, for it is actually about Nothingness, not any orthodox interpretation of God. It explores the experiences of the great enlightened sages from around the world, and how the reality that they awakened to is in fact Nothingness or Non-being. In some instances, this Nothingness is what mystics—not ordinary "religious" people—call God. Other times they call it Nirvana (*Nibbana*), *Atman, Moksha, Tao.*

In addition to many more, too numerable to mention, these figures include Shakyamuni Buddha, the authors of the *Upanishads*, Meister Eckhart, Moses Maimonides, John Scotus Erigena, Jacob Boehme, Lao Tzu, Nisargadatta Maharaj, Papaji, all of whom attest, to some degree or another, that the ultimate or highest reality is Nothingness. To borrow from some of the great spiritual traditions, Nirvana is Nothingness; Tao is Nothingness; Brahman is Nothingness; the Absolute is Nothingness.

This book was written for people who want to realize Nothingness, not for those who already think they understand God. Ideally, it should serve as a sledgehammer to demolish opinions, not create new ones.

While Nothingness may sound negative, just as the word "lack" usually does, it is the exact opposite. The world of objects is limited, Nothingness is not. Take a chair, for instance. Ordinarily speaking, we would all agree that a chair is only a chair; it is not any of the countless multitude of things *that are not a chair*. Its form circumscribes it, preventing it from being an orange or a dolphin or a turkey sandwich. Now *that* is limitation, and yet we cling to forms as if they possessed ultimate value. This is simply the result of ignorance and delusion.

Absolute Nothingness, on the other hand, is limitless, pregnant with infinite potential. For this reason, we cannot truly say that Nothingness lacks 'anything', as it is utterly *beyond* the limitations of form.

Nothingness is the very basis for reality itself, for there are simply no 'things' that can exist without or outside of Nothingness.

Nothingness makes 'being' and existence possible. In the immortal words of the Chuang Tzu, commonly regarded as the co-founder of Taoism, "The ten thousand things come forth from Nothing. Being cannot create being out of being. Inevitably it must come forth from Nothing" (Chen 89, Watson 257).

When spiritual seekers from theistic cultures realize Nothingness, they often call it "God," or—to differentiate it from the mythological Creator God—"Godhead." Based upon my own experience, "Nothingness," or its shortened form "Nothing," is a much more fitting word than "God" is.[3] After all, "Nothingness" does not have the same clumsy connotations attached to it as "God" does. No one has ever killed someone over the word "Nothingness," but the same cannot be said about "God."

.

---

[3] I will, however, use all three terms interchangeably throughout the book, for stylistic variation, and at times to emphasize one shade of meaning over another.

One of the greatest teachings of *Advaita Vedanta*, a Vedic path to realizing God based on the mystical *Upanishads*, is often overlooked. It states that, not only is our true nature identical with God, but that we are all fundamentally aware of this. We seek happiness as a surrogate because mundane pleasures mirror the greatest bliss imaginable, which is realizing our true nature. We have an intuitive sense of our own vastness and freedom, but in our confusion, we pursue limited forms of happiness such as sensory pleasures, wealth, fame, and so forth.

If we extend this further, we understand that every person has an intuitive sense of Nothingness. Nothingness need not be taught to people, for we all possess a visceral, existential understanding of non-being. In fact, if there is one thing that terrifies people the most, it is non-being. The mind reels at the mere suggestion of non-existence.

Blankness, oblivion, silence, darkness, all of these represent humanity's greatest fear—the imagined annihilation of life and beingness itself.

To illustrate this: a Catholic friend of mine once asked me, "What would you prefer, an eternity in Hell or non-existence?"

I considered the question, but before I could answer, he added solemnly, "I'd take Hell," and shivered at the mere idea of oblivion. He would rather suffer in eternal damnation than not exist. I'm sure he's not alone in that regard.

This existential terror of annihilation is so deeply rooted in our psyches that if you so much as mention the word "Nothingness" in spiritual circles, you are likely to be branded a heretic or worse, a nihilist. This is because, while people have an intuitive sense of Nothingness, they do not intellectually understand it.

They condemn it because they fear it, instinctively assuming that Nothingness is an attack on the very basis of their lives, upon existence, and that nothing could be more blasphemous than Nothingness. As we shall soon see, this stems from mistaking Nothingness as the opposite of existence, rather than as *the very basis of it*, as is the actual case.

12

This view is extremely ironic since Nothingness inherently plays such an integral, intuitive role in our sense of self. For instance, ask a small child what happens to people when they die or what they themselves were before they were born. Invariably, you will receive an answer like "Nothing" or "Nobody." That's because children have not yet formed an attachment to the notion of what adults call 'being' or 'existence', and therefore they do not consider Nothingness the opposite of 'being' in the way that so many adults mistakenly do. They understand that there is an intimate relationship between our sense of self or beingness and Non-being.

This is why Zen and Taoist masters so often instruct us to return to being a child. It is an invitation to return to the innocence and freedom of Nothingness—because becoming Nobody or Nothing is the most liberating thing we can do.

The Chinese understand Nothingness far deeper than most other cultures or people do. It took the genius of the Chinese mind, in the form of Taoism and Ch'an Buddhism, rooted so deeply in the organic and earthy spirit embodied by nature, to realize that "something" cannot come from "something" else; "something" can only come from Nothing. As the *Tao Te Ching* teaches, Nothing is the empty source and groundless, creative Ground of all existence: "All things are born of being; being is born of nonbeing [Nothingness]" (Feng Chapter 40).

Although this present book is not interested in cosmogony, in order to truly understand the nature of Nothingness (or God), we must realize its creative capacity. For its creative function—what Nothingness actually *does* or more accurately, allows to happen—offers a clearer understanding of Nothingness than trying to define what Nothingness actually *is*, because all that can be said in that respect is what Nothing *isn't*.

Nothingness, or Non-being, *precedes* being in the sense that 'being' depends upon Non-being to exist. For this reason, we can also refer to Nothingness as Non-being with a capital "N," to differentiate it from ordinary non-being, as in a description of say...the current state of Babylon today. Babylon simply...*isn't*.

This non-being is not the same as Absolute Non-being, which is Nothingness, the dark, nebulous, creative womb and nurturer of all existence.

People suffer because they don't understand Nothing, and therefore they misunderstand 'being' too. They incorrectly place 'being' *ahead* of or *above* 'Non-being' because they don't realize the difference between the great 'Non-being' and simple 'non-being.'

For most people, 'being' is the *sine qua non* of existence, even serving as a synonym for the latter. But reality is composed of both 'being' and 'Non-being', where 'Non-being' acts as the ground of 'being.' 'Being' then arises spontaneously from Nothingness.

But since people conflate 'non-being' and Non-being—thus failing to recognize 'Non-being' altogether—they mistake 'Non-being' as the opposite of 'being.' Non-being or Nothingness then represents a lack or deficit; from this perspective, Nothingness appears to be the *lack* of being rather than its basis, as the case actually is.

Nothingness is not the same as the nothing that a bankrupt man has in the bank. The former Nothing precedes 'being' altogether. It is the vibrant void from which all of existence continuously springs.

Most theists think only of 'being' (perhaps called 'Being') and existence, symbolized, of course, by God, the Supreme Being, and His creation. However, they completely misunderstand Nothingness, assuming that it is incomplete, bleak, barren, and even evil, as in a spiritual and existential vacuum or void.

Paul Tillich, the famous Christian theologian, expresses this position when he writes, "Nonbeing is dependent on the being it negates.... The ontological status of nonbeing as nonbeing is dependent on being. The character of the negation of being is determined by that in being which is negated" (40).

Tillich fails to understand the limits of 'being', as well as the infinitude of Non-being. He conflates non-being with Non-being, and in doing so, erases the latter. For him, non-being is dead, sterile, and stifling.

This position believes that 'beingness' constitutes God—that the final or ultimate truth is the pure presence of a transcendent Being who created all of existence. This view is very common among theologians and even ordinary religious people. In fact, I would wager that most people who believe in God would accept this view.

But they could not be any further from the truth. For while 'being' is more visible, occupying the foreground of our lives, Non-being serves as the ultimate background or base, even of 'being' itself.

Huang Po, one of the most celebrated and honored Ch'an (Zen) masters of all time, clearly states, "The Dharmakaya is the Void and...the Void is the Dharmakaya" (Blofeld 41). In the terms of our present conversation, this means that the God, the ultimate or final principle in the universe, is Non-being or Nothingness, the Void with a capital "V." Here, Non-being is understood, not only to to be fundamental to reality, but synonymous with the highest principle in Buddhism, the Dharmakaya.

In a complete reversal of Tillich's point of view, Nothingness actually functions as the basis of 'being', not its opposite. Without Non-being, there could be no 'being.' 'Being', meaning 'existence', and 'becoming', or 'change', can be understood as the trunk and limbs of a tree, respectively. Manifesting from Nothingness, they come and go like the seasons, with no reality independent of Nothingness.

Nothingness, on the other hand, is the roots from which both 'being' and 'becoming' arise. It is the dark, hidden, unknowable source. As the unmanifest, Non-being neither 'is' nor 'becomes.'

It is fecund and dynamic, yet unmoving; creative and vital, yet utterly empty. Limitless, boundless, vast potential.

Beyond sight, sound, smell, taste, touch, mind, and form, Nothingness nourishes, sustains, and supports all of existence. It is the mysterious, exhaustless womb of 'being.'

- 4 -

Contrary to what modern science teaches us, something cannot come from something else; something can only come from Nothing.[4] As Lao Tzu writes, "The ten thousand things are born of being. / Being is born of not being [Nothing]." All awakened ones understand this.

However, this does not mean that there is some void of Nothingness located somewhere in deep space that spits out atoms like a matter factory. We are not talking about creationism in any traditional sense. Rather, what this means is that Nothingness frees 'being' to become, transform, and evolve. In short, it allows 'being' *to be* in the first place.

For 'being' is self-contained, incapable of reaching beyond itself; while Non-being is fertile, creative, and *all*-encompassing. Forms are limited by their shape; Nothingness is infinite, all-pervading, and ceaselessly interpenetrating: "it is intangible and elusive, and yet within is image...elusive and intangible, and yet within is form...is dim and dark, and yet within is essence" (Feng, Chapter 21).

Light, like 'being', narrows and defines, whereas the darkness of Non-being brims with potential and infuses life with possibility.

Nothingness is the great numinous silence that precedes 'being.' It is the female principle of "primordial Emptiness" from which the masculine 'beingness' derives, for "only the [feminine] 'Nothing' can keep on dispensing; only Nothing is inexhaustible" (Chen 92, 94). Plainly stated, "Nothing is more ultimate than Being" (95).

This is because 'being' is actualized Nothing. Jewish scholar Daniel C. Matt writes,

> *Ayin* [Nothingness] is a window on the oneness
> that underlies and undermines the manifold
> appearance of the world. The ten thousand things
> we encounter are not as independent or

---

[4] This is not a refutation of the principle of mass conservation, which explains how energy and matter transfer. Instead, Nothingness actually allows for all of 'being' to exist, and thus underlies all physical laws. Nor is this an origins myth in disguise.

17

fragmented as they seem. There is an invisible
matrix, a swirl that generates and recycles being.
One who ventures into this depth must be
prepared to surrender what he knows and is, what
he knew and was. The ego cannot abide *ayin*; you
cannot wallow in nothingness. In *ayin*, for an
eternal moment, boundaries disappear. *Ayin*'s
"no" clears everything away, making room for a
new "yes."(47)

'Being' narrows or instantiates the infinite potential or Nothingness. For this reason,
Non-being is not the opposite of 'being', but its very fount and lifeblood.

Nothingness is not sheer blankness, yet neither is it being-ness the way that we ordinarily understand existence; it is the source and true nature of all beings. This is the "vast emptiness, nothing holy" of Bodhidharma, the legendary founder of Ch'an, Sŏn, and Zen Buddhism.

Consciousness is neither present nor absent in Nothingness, for Nothingness is actually the *root* of consciousness. In truth, there is no such thing as consciousness; there is only Nothingness.

Consciousness is instantiated Nothingness, as is all of existence.

Frightened dullards, clinging to notions of existence, call Nothingness "nihilism," unaware that Nothing is the exact opposite of deathly sterility; Non-being is the great womb from which everything arises, abides, and eventually returns. From a Buddhist perspective, "Emptiness is not a negative idea, nor does it mean mere privation, but as it is not in the realm of names and forms, it is called emptiness, or nothingness, or the Void" (Suzuki 60).

Sunyata, as Nothingness can be called in Buddhism, or *Tao* in Taoism, sustains everything, including consciousness. It is the vast, empty void of Non-existence that the Buddha calls Nirvana, meaning "extinction" of all 'being.' It is what Nisargadatta Maharaj points to when he speaks of 'Universal Consciousness' or what Huang Po calls 'Mind.'

Nothingness is *prior to* consciousness, as it is is with all phenomena. This is why Huang Po says, "Mind in itself is not mind" (Blofeld 34), meaning that the mind is truly understood only when its own emptiness is realized. For mind is Nothingness occurring *as consciousness*. When this is properly realized, mind become Mind with a capital "M," not in the sense that some latent quality has been discovered that it is somehow beyond all conditioning, like some eternal super Consciousness or Witness at the base of our mind; but in the sense that when we realize our own universality as Nothingness, we awaken to our own unlimited nature. This is what sages mean when they talk about "primordial consciousness"; it is the realization that our minds transcend beingness alone, by extending into the core nor Non-being, into Nothingness itself. The mind, in effect, is simultaneously limitless (transcendent) and

19

viscerally present (immanent). Hence, Nisargadatta calls it "Universal Consciousness" to express the insight into the universal Nothingness of our minds.

Nothingness creates, supports, animates, and eventually recalls everything, yet is not bound to any single thing. It is the stars, but not limited to them. It is the earth and all of its inhabitants, but is not confined to them.

Nothingness is the true nature of all existence. The Buddha, the Awakened One, is also called *Tathata*, meaning, "One who has arrived at suchness," *suchness* being another term for the ineffable, mysterious reality of Non-being, *sunyata,* or Nothingness.

We have risen from Nothingness, and to Nothingness we shall return. Therefore, ultimately there is no movement or nothing that ever happens, for everything is in fact Nothingness. "That which is before you is it, in all its fullness, utterly complete" (37). And yet the world continues to change and transform; the seasons come and go; people are born, grow old and die.

Nothing changes and yet everything happens.

Divinity expresses itself as an acorn, a mustard seed, a lump of coal. Humans, including their toils and vices, are all manifestations of the wondrous Nothingness. "Nothing[ness] is the inexhaustible, suprasensible power underlying all finite beings," "the emptiness from which all beings are forged" (Chen 90, 92).

Nothingness sings as birds, sighs as the wind, breathes as humans, and knows as mind. Once this is realized, there is nothing to worry about, for everything is an expression of Nothing. As the seminal Buddhist scripture, the *Heart Sutra*, says, "Form is Emptiness; Emptiness is Form."

Your truest nature is Nothingness. Mind and consciousness are in fact Nothingness. This is why Ch'an Master Linji called the Enlightened being a "person of no rank," someone who can come and go freely. "No rank" means no fixed limitation, free and vast as the sky, bound by neither 'being' nor even Non-being.

This is the infinite Nothingness of the sages.

\

Sŏn Master Seung Sahn, one of the most influential Buddhist teachers in the West, spoke of Nothingness as "Don't-know mind," "nothing-I," or "nothing-mind." When we awaken to this, "there are no mountains, no rivers, no East, West, North, or South, no God, no Buddha, nothing at all" (Mitchell 5-7).

The only way to communicate this Nothingness is to shout. Or better yet, remain silent.

While Nothingness may still sound off-putting to some readers, it shares roots with in an ancient tradition called *apophasis*, negative theology, *via negativa,* or in Sanskrit, *Neti-Neti.* These terms all refer to the same process of negating the delimited characteristics of the conventional world that we are attached to, in order to reveal the fundamental, unconditioned Absolute that precedes, underlies, and predicates the world we currently know. Although different apophatic cultures understand the Absolute in and from their own native perspectives, I think that "Nothingness" is the best referent, for reasons that I will explore below.

Apophasis is grounded in the understanding that, since we do not currently experience anything in the mundane world as God (*Neti-Neti* translates to "Not this, not that," meaning that for the common person, God is not currently found in world of objects), we must look beyond our ordinary experience to find the Absolute.

Moses Maimonides, the pre-eminent medieval Kabbalist, says, "Know that the description of God...by means of negations is the correct description...You come nearer to the apprehension...with every increase in the negations" (Matt 43). This is because our attachment to 'being' blinds us to 'being's' true nature, which is Non-being or Nothingness; therefore we must see through 'being' to its source. We do this by temporarily negating 'being' altogether, until we experience Non-being. After that, the entire world of form is seen as it truly is—as Nothingness, the very manifestation of God.

In Taoism, "the Ultimate is primarily the 'not' (*bu*) and 'no' (*wu*): [for Tao] has no name, no knowledge, no action, no desire, etc. [Nothingness] is...the negation of limitation and determination" (Chen 87). Nothingness, as we see, is free, indeterminate, and boundless; therefore, it can only be spoken about in terms of what it *is not.* However, since we do not experience the world as the body of divinity, we temporarily negate the world to reveal the unmanifest source at the heart of all 'being'.

The Buddha, speaking in similar apophatic terms, says,

> There is that sphere where there is no earth, no
> fire nor wind; no sphere of infinity of space, of

infinity of consciousness, of nothingness or even
of neither-perception-nor-nonperception; there,
there is neither this world nor the other world,
neither moon nor sun; this sphere I call neither a
coming nor a going nor a staying still, neither a
dying nor a reappearance; it has no basis, no
evolution and no support; this just this, is the end
of suffering. (*Udana* 8.1)

As in Taoism, the Buddha disqualifies everything—including common nothingness—
in order to reveal the great Nothingness beyond all explanation and predication. Once
we have negated everything, we awaken to the fertile Nothingness that is the
Buddha's Nirvana and Lao Tzu's Tao. This is the true nature of all existence, and
once we realize it, we are then free to reaffirm all of those things that we previously
negated.

In another important passage, the Buddha directly instructs his monks about how to
do this. He says,

Form, O monks, is not-self; if form were self,
then form would not lead to affliction… Feeling,
O monks, is not self...Perception, O monks, is
not-self...Mental formations, O monks, are not-
self… Consciousness, O monks, is not-self... all
those [just mentioned] must be regarded with
proper wisdom, according to reality, thus: "These
are not mine, this I am not, this is not my self."
(*Anattalakkhana Sutta*)

According to Buddha's apophatic injunction, we should negate everything that comes
across our path as "not the Absolute," especially anything that is emotionally or
psychologically charged. When we negate or discard emotions, thoughts, or objects,
firmly declaring that they are "Not the Absolute," this severs our need to control or
possess them, freeing us from the tyranny of a jealous or insecure ego.

Bear in mind that negation is a technique, not an final statement about reality. For
truthfully, *everything*—the birds, the bees, you, me, even the IRS—is an expression
of Nothingness; it is simply our relationship with the world that narrows our
experience of it. Our myopia widdles the manifest world of 'being' into discrete,
separate things that are in opposition to one another. *And if I could only get the world
to obey me, or go my way, then I would be happy.* Or so the story goes that we tell
ourselves.

Thus we suffer.

Neti-Neti teaches us that in order to realize the divine in *this* world, we must first discard everything—or to put it more precisely, we must discard how we *view* everything, or everything that we *think* we know.

As a pointer, the *Tao Te Ching* says,

> Look, it cannot be seen—it is beyond form.
> Listen, it cannot be heard—it is beyond sound.
> Grasp, it cannot be held—it is intangible.
> These three are indefinable;
> Therefore they are joined in one.
>
> From above it is not bright;
> From below it is not dark:
> An unbroken thread beyond description.
> It returns to nothingness.
> The form of the formless,
> The image of the imageless,
> It is called indefinable and beyond imagination
> (Chapter 14, translated by Feng)

This is a direct pointing through 'being' to Non-being. In a slight variation to the "Not this, not that" of traditional *Neti-Neti,* this Buddhist- and Taoist-inspired approach teaches us that our ordinary perceptions are "Not I, not me." We are not limited to our bodies or senses, sense organs, thoughts, perceptions—none of these things, either individually or even collectively, constitute 'I', 'me', or anything we can call 'mine.' Certainly we include all of these, for my arm should never be confused with your arm, but we are not limited to any, or even all, of these.

For what we truly are is the vast reservoir of Non-being that supports all of 'being'. Once this is realized, we are free to embrace *both* 'being' and Non-being, for we are limited by, and to, neither. We are the sun and stars and oceans *precisely* because of Non-being.

Returning to *Vedanta*, we see the *Brihadaranyaka Upanishad* echo this:

> This Inimitable (Brahman) is...neither gross nor
> minute, neither short nor long, neither redness nor
> color, neither shadow nor darkness, neither air nor
> ether, unattached, neither savour nor odour,
> without eyes or ears, without the vocal organ or
> mind, non-luminous, without vital force or mouth,
> without measure, and without interior or exterior.

(Nikhilananda 32)

Brahman is limited by none of these manifest characteristics; yet each is a full and complete expression of it.

The world is embodied Nothingness. But in order to fully realize this, we must first penetrate to Non-being. *Neti-Neti* or negation is a tried and true way to do that.

A common way to practice the wisdom of *apophasis* or *Neti-Neti* is to systematically negate our bodies, emotions, and minds, in order to realize our true nature as Absolute Nothingness. Look beyond the manifest to the unmanifest source.[5]

During meditation, look inward at those aspects that you commonly identify with as your 'self'; these are all finite qualities that we attach to and allow to limit us. For instance, when we feel angry, we tend to think, "I am angry," which is really a way of saying, "I am anger." Literally, I am anger; my sense of self is nothing but anger. Powerful emotions and thoughts have that power to eclipse out everything else until *only* that emotion exists.

This is extremely self-limiting and often painful.

So why do it? There are two answers to this: first, because we do not know any better (we genuinely think that our sense of self is determined by the contents of our bodies, minds, and lives); and second, because we do not even realize we are doing this. It is habitual, a bad habit like slouching or chewing with out mouths open.

Neti-Neti offers us a conscious alternative to this knee-jerk act of self-limitation. We open our sense of self by examining what we *think* we are and systematically negating it. For instance, when you are consumed with anger, examine the anger fully. Ask yourself, "Am *I* this anger?" Well, if you were then you could not even ask that question, for "anger" cannot ask questions. There must be something larger than anger to witness it and inquire about it. Therefore you are not anger, nor any other

---

[5] 'Source' here does not refer to some eternal immutable core, substratum, substantial ground or Being, but to the exact opposite. Nothingness is timeless precisely because it is Non-being, and thus not subject to change; after all, time cannot affect the formless nor that which allows time to exist in the first place. Nothingness is the source in that it allows existence to be possible, not in the literal sense that it 'creates' anything like the Abrahamic God does. It is formless, not in the mystical, ethereal way that most people imagine souls or spirits, but as the utter absence of *everything*, and thus is free of the limitations attendant with form. Paradoxically, it is this very formlessness that then allows for the world of form to be interconnected, impermanent, and, in short, to exist in the first place. Form, after all, *is* emptiness; emptiness *is* form.

passing state.

Negate them as they appear, by realizing that, in the words of the Buddha, "These are not mine, this I am not, this is not my self."

Next, inquire, "Am I my body?", followed by a thorough investigation as to where this 'I' might reside in the body. When the supposed soul or self cannot be found in or as the body, realize that "I am not my body."

What this means is that we are not limited to any *single* thing in this world—not our bodies, minds, relationships, roles, none of these can encompass who and what we truly are. This is because Nothingness, as our true nature, frees us to be everything.

Now move the inquiry to your other emotions and thoughts, your volition or will, and eventually to awareness itself. As was the case with our bodies, all of these are found to be empty of any solid or substantial 'I.' We are shocked to find that something we have taken for granted as an intuitive given—our 'I-ness' or selfhood—is actually absent.

The reason that we cannot find any 'I' is because we cannot be limited by anything that we are able to experience. For instance, our minds or awareness transcends and includes our thoughts because *we* are aware of *them*, not the other way around; thoughts can never claim to be aware of us or our awareness. That would mean our thoughts had their *own* awareness, which would amount to two awarenesses in our heads at any given moment, not to mention two selves.[6] We saw this earlier with our anger example.

Huang Po teaches,

> The Mind, which is without beginning, is unborn
> and indestructible. It is not green nor yellow, and
> has neither form nor appearance. It does not
> belong to the categories of things which exist or
> do not exist, nor can it be thought of in terms of
> new or old. It is neither long nor short, big nor
> small, for it transcends all limits, measures,
> names, traces and comparisons. (Blofeld 29)

This Mind is not some transcendent, eternal Consciousness, but rather the average everyday mind that has realized itself as Nothingness. In the words of Shen-hui, one of the most influential early Ch'an Masters, "'Seeing into one's self-nature' is 'seeing

---

[6] Boy, it's getting crowded in here!

into nothingness'" (Suzuki 31).

Huang Po, like the Buddha and other apophatic teachers, employs a series of negations, not merely because Nothingness transcends all categorization, which it does, but as a pointer to the Nothingness at the base of all phenomena. This is the "direct pointing to the mind" of Zen.

Neti-Neti is first and foremost a verb, a path to realization. It, like any tool or technique, should not be clung to as an absolute. Once negation has served its purpose, it too must be negated.

A brief detour.

Because the act of negation resembles the word "Nothing" so closely, it is easy to underestimate Nothingness and assume that once the smoke from negating has cleared, Nothingness is revealed to be in fact some entity, substance, Supreme Being, or reality *that can be spoken of in purely apophatic terms.*

No, the Absolute is really Nothingness. God is inconceivable, limitless, timeless, unconditioned, empty, markless, formless, spontaneously creative, Absolute Nothingness.

Admittedly, all verbal descriptions of the Absolute are limited, which is why we deconstruct language with language through techniques like *via negativa*. Negations such as "no color, no sound, no smell, no taste, no touch…" are, to borrow a Zen phrase, like using "blood to wash away blood." *Neti-Neti* uses language to negate language in order to reveal Absolute Nothingness.

Yet, actual Nothingness, though not a 'thing', entity, or substance, is not merely an apophatic description or directive (*Neti-Neti,* on the other hand, is). True, due to the limits of language, the word "Nothingness" can only function as a pointer, but it *is* pointing to an actual ontological reality that is experientially verifiable as Nothingness.

It's like the complete opposite of Gestalt; instead of *the whole being greater than the sum of its parts*, Nothingness' absence is greater than the sum of its negations.

In this way, Nothingness is the ultimate negation (beyond all negations). You could literally negate for eternity, every atom of the cosmos, and still not reach the depth of Non-being's emptiness. It is truly endless, and therefore completely and utterly indeterminate.

Nothingness is the utter absence of all beingness, with all that that entails.

Back to *Neti-Neti.* The next natural question in our investigation of the self becomes: *What is this 'I' who is aware? Am 'I' awareness or consciousness itself?*

And so we apply *Neti-Neti* to awareness and realize that we can never locate it. Consciousness is a moving target that can never catch hold of itself. In this sense, we can say that the mind lacks mind; it has no solid form or content. It is just clear like space.

Mind is truly empty because it has Nothingness as its true nature. This is what Zen masters mean when they say that Zen point directly to mind's true nature. It is a direct, unmediated recognition of one's own true identity as Nothingness.

In our search, all that we *do* find is a residual sense of 'I-ness' as an object, an instinctive feeling that some concrete 'I' exists, and if only we press on hard enough, we will find it.

Yet, the more we investigate this I-feeling, the more it dissolves under our scrutiny, because what appears to be 'I' is actually just more sensations in the field of our awareness—a queasy feeling in the pit of our stomach; a pervasive, indefinable physical certainty of our existence; and so forth. These are yet more insensate objects of *my* perception, it follows that 'I' am not even my sense of 'I-ness.'

At this point, most people want to scream, *So what the hell am I!*

Well, **what we are cannot be located as a 'thing'** for the sheer fact that in order for us to locate that 'thing', we must observe it. This necessarily entails a separate viewer or subject who is aware of the 'thing', which invites the natural question, how can awareness catch hold of itself? How can consciousness make an object of itself?

It can't, any more than an eye can see itself. This is because awareness is not a 'thing' to be gotten hold of, and neither are we. In fact, it is this very assumption that we are a locatable 'thing' that causes so much suffering in the first place. For why strive for fame or wealth unless there is some*one* to receive or possess it?

Neti-Neti, or any form of radical self-inquiry, reveals that there is no definitive, final 'I', not as an entity or even as awareness, to be "found."

What can be found, however, is the infinitely empty, groundless Nothingness which lies at the heart of all 'being.'

If we continue negating, we will eventually discover that we *are* Absolute Nothingness.

Anything perceptible we inevitably treat as an object separate from ourselves. To realize that everything (all of 'being') is actually Absolute Nothingness, we must transcend these forms and penetrate to the formless unmanifest that is everything's true nature. We do this by negating everything that we currently experience as NOT the Absolute. In other words, negate everything that we can perceive or sense—hear, see, smell, taste, touch, think; in short, everything that 'is' or exists—for since we experience them as objects, we invariably treat them as separate or other.

Once we have negated all 'being', what remains is Non-being, the groundless ground of existence.

As way of analogy, imagine that the Absolute is like the host of a party, and objects are its guests. The host, by its very nature, cannot be a guest at the party it is hosting any more than a symphony composer can attend her own concert as a member of the audience.[7] If we want to know whose party we are attending, but cannot find the host on our own, simply eliminate those people you know *are not* the host (the guests), until only one person remains. Whoever that is must be the host, or in the case of contemplative inquiry, the Absolute.

That is the crux of *Neti-Neti* or *apophasis.*

Taoist masters have a similar practice called *zuowang,* meaning "sitting in oblivion." Here

> one abandons outward manifestations, then one
> becomes oblivious of that which causes these
> manifestations. On the inside one is unaware that
> there is a body-self; on the outside one never
> knows there are Heaven and Earth. Only thus can
> one become fully vacant and unify with the
> changes, and there will be nothing that is not

---

[7] The analogy is not intended to imply doership or ultimate subjectivity on the part of the Absolute.

pervaded. (Kohn 17)

As both of these practices demonstrate, to find God, eliminate everything that you encounter ("outward manifestations") in the sphere of 'being', from the physical forms around you and the perceptions you experience, to your entire interior realm of imagination and conceptual thought.

Because we view everything as external objects, we do not experience the divinity in 'being.' To remedy this, treat them all as *Neti-Neti*, "Not this, not that." Paradoxically, this then liberates 'being' by uncovering its true nature, as a manifestation of Nothingness.

During formal meditation, systematically negate everything that you encounter one after another, the way a gold panner removes soil to isolate gold. "This is NOT It, that is NOT It."

Anything that can be perceived or conceived should be viewed as not final, and therefore discarded. Time, space, form, emotions, thoughts, sensations, consciousness, all of these 'exist' and therefore rely upon Nothingness.

Relinquish them and return to Nothingness.

Nothingness is the complete absence of everything that exists in the realm of 'being'; it is the formless, unborn Absolute that precedes, and allows for, all of 'being.' It is the final and ultimate predicate.

This is the Nirvana that the Buddha awakened to, Meister Eckhart's *Gottheit* (Godhead), Lao Tzu's Tao, and Nisargadatta's Absolute, *Parabrahman.*

Nirvana means 'extinguishing', as in the extinction of fire, a common analogy for desire. When we eliminate everything that we think has reality, eventually we shall arrive at that which cannot be negated because there is no 'thing-ness' to be negated.

This is primordial Nothingness.

After you have developed a certain degree of stability in returning to Nothingness, you can begin to practice during everyday life. When you find yourself attached to or drawn into a situation, enmeshed in the mire of powerful emotions, sever the false sense of ultimate reality that you have erroneously imbued the event with by realizing that whatever the situation or person or emotion is, the way that you are presently experiencing it is as an object.

And anything we experience or encounter as an object cannot be IT.

Nothingness defies all objectification. Huang Po says about this, "Our original Buddha-Nature is, in highest truth, devoid of any atom of objectivity" (Blofeld 35). This means that viewing anything as separate from us, as an object, is not "the highest truth."

Another way to gain clarity about a strong emotion or sensation, perhaps jealousy or physical pain, is to inquire where it came from. Ask:

Where was [the emotion] before it appeared?

In other words, where was the pain before you felt it?

Where was [the anger or love] before it arose?

Since everything in the phenomenal world is transient and arises dependent on conditions, nothing we can perceive or conceive has the ability to be independent or self-sufficient.

Everything originates from, resides in, and eventually returns to Nothingness.

For instance, pain cannot truly be said to be the Absolute because pain cannot exist on its own. In addition to being dependent on a physical body and nervous system to actually experience it, pain arises *from* Nothingness. Pain, along with love and joy, the Milky Way and black holes, has no existence whatsoever outside of Nothingness. But not the other way around—Nothingness does not rely upon the world of form or objects.

Rather, they are manifestations of the unmanifest. They are waves and Nothingness is the ocean. Without the ocean, there are no waves. Similarly, without Non-being there is no 'being.'

The beauty of the process is that once we arrive at Nothingness, we are free to resurrect all of the things that we just negated! Nothingness redeems ordinary life, revitalizing it with energy, clarity, and wisdom; it imbues us with freedom and passion without the anxious need to possess and control everything. Life becomes playful and light, as we realize that the entire world, from the ugliest wart to the most beautiful symphony, is an expression of the Absolute. It is the divine dance of Nothingness.

Then we no longer need to transcend the world because we understand that its true nature is Nothingness itself.

In the words of Japanese poet, Bassho, "Fleas, lice, / a horse pissing / by my bed." These are all expressions of Nothingness—fleas, lice, horse piss and all.

Imagine that you have a ledger inside of your head, like a mental encyclopedia, containing everything that you have ever learned or inferred.

Whenever you encounter an emotionally charged moment, perform this fast investigation: *Did this emotion create itself?*

The answer, of course, is *no*. It arose from Nothingness and will return to Nothingness in a short time; in fact, it even abides in Nothingness, for Nothingness is the ultimate predicate. It is present everywhere.

Once you answer *no*, you can then cross that 'item' off of your mental ledger. Put an "X" next to that entry in your mental encyclopedia: *Ok, I am now certain that 'fear' is NOT It. On to the next item...*

Another important consideration to remember is that anything we can experience is not It because It cannot be reduced to an object. So if you are not totally convinced, or perhaps the emotion is so persuasive that it keeps drawing you back in, return to your natural state of awareness as a witness and remember that if you can experience something, it cannot be It. For the Absolute can never be experienced as an object.

The goal of the practice is to disentangle ourselves from the messy emotional situations we create, by realizing that none of them are ultimately real, and are therefore unworthy of the time and worry we invest them with. It frees us to enjoy our lives without being ensnared by the temperamental vicissitudes of life. Like if we discovered that our favorite reality-TV show is actually scripted, we would no longer worry about the misfortune of our favorite stars because the events are not *really* happening.

Then we are free to enjoy the show without fear or anxiety.

The same applies to our lives—with practice, we can learn how to engage our lives fully without needing to control every aspect of them.

But until we discover Nothingness, we will be forever chasing 'things.' This practice reinforces the knowledge that none of the events or things we encounter have the absolute value that we impute upon them. So why worry about them so much?

Engaging this practice during our everyday activities is crucial to integrating and embodying our meditative insight into the fabric of our lives. *Neti-Neti* should not be relegated to the seated position or while we are on a meditation cushion; it needs to penetrate into every aspect of our lives if it is to enact true fruitful transformation. This means seeing through the sticky emotional and conceptual mire that ordinarily enmeshes us.

What is this? Is this IT?

Simply asking these questions can break the spell that strong emotions have over us; for, rather than being blindly drawn into their folds under the ruse that they are themselves absolutes, we can see through them. This places life events in their proper context—as appearances from and in Nothingness.

We have a lifetime of mental conditioning to undo, decades of grasping at possessions, people, and relationships as if they were final, absolutes all by themselves. These habits have to be systematically dismantled *every time that we encounter them*. The way to do that is to negate them as they arise.

You are not an object, and neither is God. When we fully penetrate to the true nature of 'being', we experience all existents as instantiations of the Absolute. The more skilled we become at this process, the more natural, fluid, and graceful our shift from an object-orientated mode to the freedom of Non-being will become.

Nothingness is always available to us, for it is atemporal, uncircumscribed, and all-inclusive[8]. In fact, we experience Nothingness directly every day and night.

During deep sleep, when our consciousness retreats entirely and dreams have not yet appeared, we abide as our original stateless state. Then there is only Nothingness. Our minds, for all intents and purposes, are completely absent. Without an object to be aware of, our subjective self recedes back into Nothingness. This is a return to the mind *prior to* mind, before awareness altogether.

Nothingness, dark, serene, and all-pervading.

Ask yourself, *Where do I go every night in between dreaming and waking? When my consciousness and sense of self drops away entirely, where am 'I'?*

The answer, utterly inconceivable (literally), is a direct experience of your true nature, Nothingness.

When you ask this, your mind clutches for something concrete to hold onto in order to explain how there could be a gaping hole in its beingness, but none appears. That *lack of a something* is IT—the vast, fathomless Void that Bodhidharma speaks of.

This is God. Not the jealous, Supreme Being, the mythological creator God, the wrathful deity who demands fealty and obedience; nor even the loving, personal God who sees all beings as "His" children.

This is Meister Eckhart's *Nichts* (Nothingness). Empty, markless, and signless.

---

[8] Yet it is found nowhere but here, in this present moment, the very forms that surround us—our bodies, the earth, this book.

People crave Nothingness like a newborn does its mother's milk. The Nothingness of deep sleep is "sore labor's bath, / Balm of hurt minds, great nature's second course, / Chief nourisher in life's feast" (Shakespeare 2. 2. 39-41). Although we do not remember deep sleep, we instinctively need it, for nothing in life is as refreshing as a good night's rest.

This is because it is a direct return to Nothingness. In deep sleep, when all objects of body and mind recede, when our sense of self disappears, we abide in the tranquil emptiness of pure Nothingness.

The dark enfolding womb of Nothingness constantly welcomes us home, which is why so many people seek the oblivion of drugs and alcohol. Sigmund Freud explained this as the desire to return to the oceanic state of a mother's womb, which is half right. Freud was correct about the unconscious drive for non-being, but what he, like so many others, failed to recognize is the Nothingness that precedes 'being' altogether—Absolute Non-beingness that transcends Freud's oceanic fixation.

Sri Ramana Maharshi, one of the greatest sages who ever lived, famously instructed a student to "Go back the way you came" (Osborne 60). He was pointing to the great Nothingness that precedes all of life entirely, the experience of universal Non-being that we all unconsciously are and long for.

However, we must not get seduced by language into thinking that humans' drive for Nothingness is regressive ("Go *back* the way you came"), as Freud would have us believe. It is not. Granted, many so-called "spiritual" people are more interested in finding an escape from the stress of their lives than they are in genuine insight into the Absolute; but for the fully actualized ego, the human quest for enlightenment, to know God, is an expression of humanity's upward momentum to understand its true nature as Nothingness. This is not regression, but a quest for self-realization.

We also experience Nothingness thousands of time each day. Consciousness is not a continuous stream; it's broken into millions of frames like a film reel. In between thoughts and leaps in our visual field, we can spot subtle breaks in what otherwise appears to be the fluid stream we call 'us.' Every time that we blink, shift our gaze, move our attention from one sense to another, like from sound to sight, our mind fills in these gaps, creating the illusion of continuous experience.

But this is not the case.

'Mind' or 'self' is a construct of our nervous system. If we pay close attention, we will spot these breaks.

Skeptical? Scrutinize any of your senses; I'd recommend sight because it is the one that people identify with and rely upon the most. Turn the lights on and stare at a blank surface like a blank sheet of paper or a white wall. You will notice the imperfections in your vision, blotches or floating masses of translucent color. These appear *in* your actual visual experience itself, not on your *eyes* like the vitreous floaters that hover on some people's cornea.

If you study these closely, you will discover that these spots are not hovering on your vision; they *are* your vision. This is because there is no experiencer *behind* our sensory experiences; there is only the perceptions themselves. They are, to borrow computer terminology, our human user interface.

Consciousness or awareness (I use these two interchangeably) is sorely misunderstood, for ultimately there is no such thing as consciousness in and of itself. There is no absolute entity, being, or capacity called consciousness, as if consciousness were residing on a plane of its own in some pure, intangible form; absolute subjects are a fantasy. There is no latent subject or awareness waiting to receive sensory data like a TV monitor in our heads. Consciousness always entails an object; it depends on objects to exist.

In order for awareness to occur, we must be aware *of* something. For instance, if we injured our eyes and suddenly went blind, we would have no visual awareness. The same applies to all of our other sense organs. If we were to pull the metaphorical power plug on all of our senses, including our mental faculties like imagining and reasoning, consciousness would cease, just like in deep sleep.

This means that our minds or consciousness are *produced* by or rely upon our senses, and therefore, we are actually experiencing our own nervous systems and their interpretations of sense data more than we are some hypothetical raw reality. Consciousness, then, should not and must not be placed on a pedestal as if it were unconditioned. It isn't. This approach only leads to reifying consciousness as an absolute. From there, all sorts of problems ensue. The truth is that if we did not have a body, we would no longer be conscious. Consciousness is a process just like our heartbeat and circulating blood.

Nothingness, however, is *prior to* our experiences, our senses, and consciousness, all of which arise dependent upon a myriad of other factors to exist, such as a body, oxygen, sustenance, etc. Nothingness is what allows consciousness to occur because it allows all of 'being' to be.

Nisargadatta's Universal Consciousness or Huang Po's One Mind emerges when our ordinary mind realizes its bottomless ground as Nothingness. Enlightenment is the union of conditioned consciousness and the illimitable, inexhaustible source of everything, as the mind gazes into its own boundless source. What follows is the recognition that, just as our minds are Nothingness, so too is all of existence. Reality, or 'being', is instantiated Nothingness; the world is a manifestation of unmanifest Non-being.

Just as in deep sleep, Nothingness can be experienced *in between* the spaces in our consciousness. Dark, vast, empty, still, silent, but infinitely receptive and supportive, womb-like.

The more often that we return to zero, so to speak, the more stable our ability to abide in the emptiness of Non-being will grow. That is realizing God right here, right now—by becoming the Nothing that we and all beings truly are.

Nonduality is the teaching that everything is one, non-separate whole. From the viewpoint of nonduality, individuality is an illusion that causes beings to suffer because they feel separate from the rest of the world. As so-called separate beings, we strive to exert our will upon an uncooperative world, against which we feel pitted; the inevitable result is anger, frustration, anguish, jealousy, confusion, resentment, and many other painful thoughts and emotions.

The realization that we are never separate from the world, that reality is one seamless whole, dissolves our suffering because we no longer feel fragmented or incomplete. After all, why strive for fame or wealth when you understand that, since all beings are actually connected, you do not lack anything in the first place?

This is a wonderful realization, but it is not the final word.

A major shortcoming with much of the nonduality pervading the modern spiritual marketplace is that it seldom acknowledges the Nothingness which permits 'being' in the first place. Awareness, Being, Presence—or some variation or combination of the three—and interconnectedness, seem to represent the extent of what modern nonduality is interested in.

Nothingness, however, transcends even nonduality; for while the nondual whole encompasses everything—all of 'being', in fact—it does not include Non-being, which precedes and acts as the very basis of 'being' itself. Imagine: if nonduality, the interconnected matrix of all 'being', including mind or consciousness, were represented by an oil painting, then Nothingness is the canvas upon which the picture resides.

Nothingness pervades the entire nondual universe; it is the principle that permeates everything. In other words, Nothingness allows nonduality to occur in the first place, just as it does 'being.'

The reason that the human body, mind, consciousness/awareness, interpenetrate is because Nothingness allows them to exist—or rather, they exist *as* manifest Nothingness.

This must be realized.

Experiencing nonduality is not yet Enlightenment. We must penetrate deeper, past all sense of 'being', to the canvas below the paint to realize our and all beings' true nature as boundless Nothingness. When that happens, ordinary mind becomes the Mind of the sages.

Buddha Mind, then, is the mind's recognition of its own empty, groundlessness, not as some eternal supreme principle called Awareness, but as the very living, conscious embodiment of Nothingness in *this* world, at this very moment.

It is not an exaggeration to say that consciousness is the act of Nothingness being aware.

To know ultimate Nothingness, jettison *everything*. That means the world, your body, mind, ideas, beliefs, saviors, prophets, Buddhas, and even consciousness itself. Everything in the manifest realm must go.[9]

In order to look Nothingness in the eyes, you must cease being this limited 'I' and become Nothing. The 18th-century Hasidic rabbi Dov Baer, agrees, saying

> One must think of oneself as *ayin* [nothingness]
> and forget oneself totally...Then one can
> transcend time, rising to the world of thought,
> where all is equal: life and death, ocean and dry
> land.. . . Such is not the case when one is attached
> to the material nature of this world.. . . If one
> thinks of oneself as something...God cannot
> clothe [It]self in him, for [God] is infinite, and no
> vessel can contain [It], unless one thinks of
> oneself as *ayin* [nothingness]. (Matt 45-6)

Rabbi Baer is encouraging us to penetrate to the deepest core of our being, to its base, to Nothingness. This experience is beyond even nonduality, for anything that exists *solely* in the realm of 'being' is by definition limited, determined, and circumscribed. Nothingness, on the other hand, is limitless, indeterminate, and all-pervading precisely because it is not the opposite of 'being', but in fact being-ness' bottomless ground.

In this sense, Nothingness is the field upon which nonduality actually occurs.

---

[9] As I have said before, but want to stress again, this negational approach is provisional. Eventually, once Nothingness is fully realized, all of these are recognized as actualized forms of Nothingness. Then we are free to embrace them.

Shankara, commonly viewed as the father of *Advaita Vedanta,* famously says, "Brahman is the Reality; the universe is *maya* [illusion]." This means that form—not just differentiated form, but *form* itself—needs to be penetrated in order for one to realize the ultimate truth.

Brahman means It, the completely un-predicatable, what I and the medieval Dominican sage Meister Eckhart call Nothingness. Nisargadatta, in my opinion the greatest sage of the past hundred years, says,

> The world is your direct experience, your own observation. All that is happening is happening at this level, but I am not at this level. I have dissociated myself from *Sattva Guna,* beingness.
>
> The Ultimate state in spirituality is that state where no needs are felt at any time, where nothing is useful for anything. That state is called *Nirvana, Nirguna,* that which is the Eternal and Ultimate Truth. The essence and sum total of this whole talk is called *Sat-guru Parabrahman,* that state in which there are no requirements.
>
> After the dissolution of the universe, when no further vestige of creation was apparent, what remained is my perfect state. All through the creation and dissolution of the universe, I remain ever untouched. I have not expounded this part: my state never felt the creation and dissolution of the universe. I am the principle which survives all the creations, all the dissolutions. This is my state, and yours, too, but you don't realize it because you are embracing your beingness. (Dunn 10)

As Shankara would say, we can never pinpoint what Brahman *is* as an object, for to assign labels to it, even ones as slippery as 'awareness' or 'emptiness', is to limit it. We cannot even say something as trite as, "Brahman simply *is*," for that circumscribes Brahman inside of the notion of 'being', which naturally invites its opposite, 'non-being.' And as seen above, Nisargadatta completely eradicates the possibility that Brahman is 'being.' Meister Eckhart resolves this, as best as one can within language, by saying that "God is Nothing."

Admittedly, this, like all statements about the Absolute, is a pointer at best, and limited by language and concepts; but I find that 'Nothing' is a better pointer than others because 'Nothingness' amputates thinking entirely. For what *is* Nothingness? How can the mind imagine Nothingness? Any attempt leaves us clutching for some*thing* to grasp hold of, but Nothingness, by its very nature, defies conceptualization.

That feeling of utter empty Non-beingness *is* Nothingness.

Shankara's ultimate goal, like the Buddha's and most contemplative traditions, is to get beyond all concepts, for ultimately they are all *maya* or illusory.

Nisargadatta says, "From 'Nothingness', this 'I-am-ness' has appeared" (Powell 147), again suggesting that not only is the Absolute *prior to* our sense of self, but it is beyond all predicates, for what could Nothingness possibly depend upon? Nothingness is the ultimate predicate, the perennial background upon which all existents abide.

In order to realize this Absolute, we must abandon all concepts, which is why "Nothingness" proves to be such a useful tool—it eradicates conceptualization altogether, for the sheer fact that Nothingness is impossible to imagine. Instead, it must be experienced. This requires a radical shift from our attachment to 'being', which operates in the foreground of our experience, to Non-being, which functions invisibly as the background.

Nisargadatta says, "Everything is beingness, but I, the Absolute, am *not* that" (Dunn 9, my italics). And, "Consciousness is time flowing continuously. But I, the Absolute, will not have its company eternally because consciousness is time bound. When this beingness goes, the Absolute will not know 'I Am.' Appearance and disappearance, birth and death, these are the qualities of beingness; they are not your qualities" (Dunn 11). Whatever Nisargadatta is—what we all are, in fact—he is clearly *not* beingness.

So what is he? This is the ultimate question, whose answer is what "Nothingness" points to.

To answer with words would insult the question.

In true apophatic form, we cannot say what God *is*—for that objectifies God—only what it *isn't.* God is not a soul or spirit or consciousness or mind or body or any other of the thousands of things that we might think It is. These all limit God.

God is none of these things; it transcends, yet serves as the basis for, all of them.

"Nothingness" will have to do as a pointer.

Interlude

The Nirvana Gospel

God, the unconditioned, unborn Absolute,
cannot be found in form, feelings, perceptions, impulses, or
consciousness.
Thus it is called Nothingness.
It cannot be sensed with eyes, ears, nose, tongue, body, or mind;
it has no color, no sound, no smell, no taste, no touch, or any
form knowable by mind.
It cannot be conceived by thought or perceived by the senses.

Cast them aside like ash in order to fully realize Nothingness
beyond form and mind, conditions and causation.
When all of existence has been transcended,
the Absolute shall reveal itself as
primordial Nothingness.

Every being and atom exists inside of,
and as expressions of, the Absolute;
it is the womb of all phenomena.
All existents are manifestations of Nothingness,
even so-called 'defilements.'
Their true nature is the same as that of
all of the enlightened sages.
Thus, there are no hindrances;
the Great Way is always wide open.

Form arises from Nothingness,
exists as Nothingness,
and returns to Nothingness.
Infinitely expansive, Nothingness supports everything.
Thus, when sages see form, they see Nothing.
Form is Nothingness, Nothingness is form.

Nothingness transcends all categories and dualities:
It is unborn and undying, neither changing nor eternal.
It is formless and boundless; neither self nor other, Self nor no-self.
It is beyond will or volition, neither an entity nor a substance.
It is tranquil and serene, neither moving nor inert.
It is markless and empty, beyond pureness and defilements.

Nothingness precedes subject and object, existence and non-existence.
It is unconditioned and all-pervading.

Awakening to Nothingness marks the highest
and most complete realization,
the marrow of all sages.

Those who know Nothingness are awakened;
those who do not are deluded.

You can awaken to the unconditioned in an instant:
simply negate all that you can see, hear, taste, touch,
feel, and think.

THAT which remains, which cannot be negated, is Absolute Nothingness.

Beyond all colors, sounds, smells, flavors, sensations, experiences,
thoughts, is total Non-being.

All that can be said about it is that it is NOT.

Nothingness needs no cultivation,
for like the sky, it cannot be stained nor defiled.
It is numinous, without a second, which, like infinite space,
cannot be born nor perish, be added to nor subtracted from.
It is your and all beings' true face,
the mother of all awakened beings.

Realize this and you will transcend all delusions, karma, and attachments,
and return to your own pristine, immediate nature,
which is none other than Nothingness,
from which, in truth, you have never departed.

All phenomena are expressions of Nothingness,
and thus they continuously proclaim:

Nothingness is the true nature of all beings.
To realize that I and all of existence are Nothing is freedom and enlightenment.

- 22 -

Often we hear spiritual teachers say, "You are what you are looking for."

What rubbish! The entire reason that we are seeking in the first place is because what we are looking for is really *an idea*, although we don't know it yet.

The problem is that we think that we already know what we *are* or what we are looking for. In our minds, it is some *thing*—call it spirit, soul, God, consciousness, awareness, Christ, Buddha nature, whatever—that we must locate or unveil, and once we do that, all of our problems will vanish. Then we can go about the rest of our lives, happy and content with the car, the dog, and the family.

But these are just ideas that we have fixated upon.

You are not some *thing* that needs finding, nor are you the seeker. It would be incorrect even to say that you are Nothing, for that implies that there is a 'you' in the first place.

Wei Wu Wei writes,

> Why are you unhappy?
> Because 99.9 per cent
> Of everything you think,
> And of everything you do,
> Is for yourself —
> And there isn't one.
> —*Ask The Awakened*

There is simply Nothingness. That is all that can be said. There is no 'you' involved. We must demolish the idea that there is some 'I' who hears and sees and smells and makes decisions. There simply is no such a thing. Nor is there a body.

It is this very insistence that there is some 'I' which creates the search in the first place. Erase the 'I' and the search immediately becomes meaningless.

All that there is is Nothingness. The physical world is a passing show like pictures on a TV. That is the manifest realm.

Nothingness is the unmanifest, the TV screen itself. To realize it, simply negate everything you can see, hear, smell, taste, touch, think, or experience. As Nisargadatta puts it, if you can remember something, it isn't It. Anything cognizable, perceivable, or experienceable in any way is not It. These are objects, and the Absolute cannot be experienced objectively.

If you think that this sounds negative or world-renouncing, then you must believe that there is a world to renounce.

There isn't; there is simply Nothingness.

Negate the so-called "world" and you will realize for yourself. The only catch is that 'you' won't be there to enjoy it; for in order to experience Nothingness, you must become Nothingness. That means the extinction of the illusory 'I.'

Consciousness depends on the body. Being depends on the body. Presence depends on the body. Before you were born, where was consciousness, being, and presence? When your body perishes, where will consciousness, being, and presence go?

The mind, emotions, and all experiences depend on the body. Our entire lives and everything we can imagine depends on the body.

They are bubbles passing along on the stream of the body. When the water dries up, the bubbles vanish.

You are not the water nor the bubbles.

You are the great Nothingness from which all forms, experiences, thoughts, awareness and consciousness emerge, dance, and eventually retreat.

Existence and 'being' arise from Non-being like momentary flickers of light from the dark womb of deep space, ripples upon the infinite ocean of Nothingness.

Existence resides inside of time; Nothingness makes time and change possible. The manifest is subject to change; the unmanifest is changeless, undying, and unborn. Beingness is time-bound; Nothingness is timeless, spaceless, changeless, yet is none other than the source of time, space, and the entire universe.

People want to hear and say that the Absolute, God, is Awareness, Presence, Being, Love, or some other term that points to something that appears graspable.

It's not.

Forget all of those things, for they are guests; instead, seek the host who invited them. That is your true nature. That is God

Nothingness precedes everything, including awareness, presence, and 'being.' It is what makes them all possible.

If you can say what God *is*, God is not *that*. God is none of those things.

God is NOT. Period. No predication.

"Nothingness" should act as a vacuum to remove all concepts of what God *is*. God does not "exist." Nothingness transcends existence; 'being' arises from Non-being.

Do not get mired inside of terms; God is beyond all of them. "[Nothingness] implies the God beyond God, the power that is closer and further than what we call 'God.' It symbolizes the fullness of being that transcends being itself" (Matt 47).

Existence depends on non-existence, not the other way around.

To realize Nothing, become Nothing. Negate all of 'being' and see that which is Not. Then negate Nothingness too.

Don't stop short at awareness; God is NOT that. Awareness is a portal through which we must pass to realize Nothingness.

Ordinary consciousness arises from Nothingness, abides inside of Nothingness, and returns to Nothingness.

Consciousness depends entirely upon the physical body. When the body dies, awareness vanishes. It is a passing state that dependent entirely upon the body.

But one thing does not depend upon the body. What is that one thing? What is it that the body and the entire cosmos depend upon?

When you are in deep, dreamless sleep, where has your awareness gone? Just as your sense of 'I' drops off, so does your consciousness. That which remains is your true face, the faceless face of God.

Use awareness to discover Nothingness, but do not venerate the instrument itself. Awareness comes and goes; it can be sharp or dull, bright or hazy, attentive or sluggish.

The Absolute can be none of those things. It is completely unconditioned, unperturbed, silent, and still.

If you wonder, "Then who is it that is aware of the Absolute?", then you are miles away from it. You have fallen into a pit of quicksand. As Huang Po says, "begin to reason about it and you at once fall into error" (Blofeld 29).

Zen understands Nothingness perfectly, completely unmediated by concepts.

One need look no further than the most famous koan—a device used by a teacher to point to Nothingness—called "Zhaozhou's dog." In it, a monk asks Ch'an Master Zhaozhou if a dog has Buddha Nature.

Rather than entertain a philosophical answer, such as "yes" or "no," Zhaozhou *points directly* to Buddha nature itself.

"*Wu*," he says, Chinese for "Nothing." His word hits a bulls eye. Buddhahood, a direct seeing into the groundless ground of reality, like God and the Tao, *is* to become Nothingness, which is what Zhaozhou conveys to the young monk.

"*Wu!*"

The challenge for Zen students is to penetrate into the heart of this koan of all koans, to embody with flesh, blood, mind, and heart, the Nothingness that Zhaozhou expresses.

Students must *become* Nothing, realize the Nothingness that has always pervaded their being. Breathe Nothing as Nothing, eat Nothing as Nothing, be Nothing as Nothing.

But this is not a breakthrough to a special state; this is our original face—the vast, creative, formless Nothingness that transcends, and yet manifests, *as* time, form, and space.

Nagarjuna, often hailed as the second Buddha, was an unrivalled philosopher; but even more impressively, he used logic to demolish both logic *and* delusion. The Middle Way, his systematic approach, awakened students to the Absolute by destroying all categories of supposed existence until only an unmediated, direct experience of nonconceptual reality remained.

It is a fourfold negation that eradicates everything in its path—objects, subjects, times, space, motion, you name it—even, and especially, any underlying ontology that someone might cling to, such as self, presence, consciousness, or beingness. What's left, of course, is Nothingness, or in Buddhist terms, Tathata or Suchness.

Here's how it works.

Through a merciless gauntlet of reasoning, Nagarjuna demonstrates that things cannot be said to exist, but neither can they be said *not* to exist. Continuing, he evinces how things cannot be said to both exist and not exist, for that is clearly irrational. And lastly, things cannot be said not to exist *nor not* to exist.

This negational tetralemma cuts off all avenues of conceptual escape, emptying all of our mental categories until all that remains is an unmediated experience of things *as they are*. In Nagarjuna's words, this is emptiness or *sunyata*, the extinction of all concepts.

In the words of Joseph Gikatilla, "The depth of primordial being . . . is called *ayin* [nothingness]. . . If one asks, 'What is it?' the answer is, *'Ayin,'* that is, no one can understand anything about it.. . . It is negated of every conception" (Matt 44).

The final step is to empty emptiness itself, leaving...*Nothingness*.

Just as with *Neti-Neti*, Nagarjuna's method pulls the mental carpet out from beneath us, until, like the wind of ignorance knocked out of us as we crash onto our backs, we inhale a fresh, *pre*conceptual lungful of air.

Ahh, the rich and free smell of boundless Nothingness.

Silence speaks the name of God, Listen, and you will hear it. Meister Eckhart says, "It is in the stillness, in the silence, that the word of God is to be heard. There is no better approach to this Word than through stillness, through silence."

John Cage understood this very intimately. Listen to his composition 4'33" and hear for yourself.

Where would humanity be without zero? 0 makes our entire lives possible. All complex mathematics—geometry, calculus, trigonometry, statistics—owe zero homage. Without 0, modern engineering, architecture, pharmacy, medicine, and science would all be inconceivable.

Zero is numerical Chaos, seething, teeming with protean potentiality. The root of all numbers, zero gives selflessly, endlessly. Empty, yet suffused with the dark, silent dynamism of the great void womb, it animates the imagination and human spirit.

0

God(dess) is zero, the fertile number of not-yet-happened and unlimited soon-to-be's.

Zero is present in every number, hidden, a consummate companion and partner.

1 is always 1, never 2 nor 5; and 1,000,000, large as it is, can only ever be 1,000,000. However, 0 can be anything and everything.

Zero is Nothingness, the muse of artists and poets, the fertile vision of mystics. All poems are odes to zero; all paintings and sculptures are monuments inspired by Nothingness.

0 is as holy as motherhood.

Stillness, the act of doing nothing. When we do nothing, we do everything. Meditation, sitting still and doing nothing, is the most important thing we can do. It is embodying divinity with our hearts, minds, and every inch of our bodies. Sitting still and silent, being zero, is fully actualizing Nothingness.

God is silence. Sit still and realize that.

A helpful way to understand Nothingness is in the same way as we do the Chinese word *Tao,* which translates to "The Way" in English. When left untranslated, the word "Tao" immediately summons to mind a thing, the same way as the word "God" invites the sense of an entity; however, when we translate "Tao" as "The Way," its meaning blooms like a flower. Instead of an insensate force of nature, as the word "Tao" often implies, "The Way" suggests a path to be engaged. It is suffused with energy, and entails action on our part.

In this sense, *Tao* can be understood as a verb, something we *do.* The same can be said about Nothing. If we Nothing, as the ancient Taoist sages prompt us to do—as in *wu wei* (無 爲), the act of "non doing," or better still, *wei wu wei* (爲 無 爲), "doing non-doing"—then we return to Nothing *when we Nothing* (used as a verb, like "We run," "We ski," "We Nothing").[10]

"We Nothing," where "Nothing" acts as a verb, is about as close to the Taoist *wu wei* as we can get. Soon the "we" disappears and there is simply "Nothing."

Taoists recommend just taking

> the position of non-action (*wu wei*) and all things
> unfold naturally. Let your body and limbs fall
> away, expel perception and intellect, leave
> relations and things behind in oblivion. Become
> mystically one with the immense and boundless;
> release your mind and free your spirit. Be silent
> and without an active spirit soul [that interacts
> with the world], and the ten thousand things will
> each return to their root. (Kohn 20)

Whose root, of course, is Nothingness.

This is not a dead state, but the exact opposite. Returning to Nothingness infuses our

---

[10] I say "We Nothing" rather than "We *do* Nothing" because the former evokes an intimacy between the subject "we" and the verb "Nothing" that is lost when "Nothing" is used as the direct object in the latter clause.

life with vitality and a sense of freedom from the constraints and limits of 'being', which remained hitherto unimaginable. We shrug off the burden of "having things to do" and are free simply "to do" with the lightness and airiness of nothing holding us down.

Nothing then washes the dishes. *Nothing* sends an email. *Nothing* draws the bathwater. This is the Taoist *wei wu wei*—doing nothing, doing everything. We are fully engaged in the thick of our lives without our hyper-self-consciousness getting in our way.

Then it is the dishes washing the dishes *and* Nothing washing Nothing.

How marvelous! How liberating!

We all should aspire to Nothingness.

Peter Gibbons expresses this perfectly in the comedy classic *Office Space*. When asked what he did instead of coming to work on Saturday, he says, "I did nothing. I did absolutely nothing, and it was everything I thought it could be." And he is the happiest he has ever been in his entire life, all due to Nothing.

Because in the end, as Peter discovers, doing Nothing is doing everything.

The worst things we can do with Nothingness is to reify it. That's when medicine turns to poison.

When I teach my Buddhist students about emptiness, I like to call it a verb, as in *to empty*. Emptiness is not a thing or substance underlying forms; nor is it a vacuum-like absence inside of them.

Emptiness, properly employed, demolishes views so that we can experience life directly, unmediated by all of the conceptual clutter that ordinarily festoons our minds and lives.

Empty ourselves of our attachment to our bodies, our lives, goals, anxieties, frustrations, story lines…

What emerges is a spaciousness. Some might call this *emptiness*, but that is adding words where none are needed. "Emptying emptiness" is the act of letting go of any fixed, solid view of emptiness; it is the liberation of oneself from yet another conceptual prison, this time called "emptiness."

The same should be done to Nothingness.

Nothingness needs to be negated, transcended, and emptied so as to avoid reifying it into a golden calf. Nothingness is not a thing, a substance, entity, or some sort of spiritual ether that animates us all like George Lucas's The Force. It is not intelligent, willful, or alive.

Neither is Nothingness a conceptual or abstract category. It is directly apprehensible.

Nothingness is NOT; it is ungraspable because it is NOT. It is utterly inexhaustible and completely indeterminate. Because it is formless, Nothingness is never final or "done." If we ever think that we "have it," then we do not; what we have then is an idea, which is the surest sign that we have reified Nothingness.

Nothingness, properly understood, defies reification, for by definition it is NOTHING and therefore can never be singularly found in the same way we do our missing wallet.

It cannot be directly pinpointed in the realm of 'being', yet neither is it located in some alternate dimension.

And yet the only place it can be known is here, in this very world of form and 'being'. This paradox is not meant to be resolved, but rather actualized through the realization that Nothingness is form, form is Nothingness.

As the living manifestation of the hidden unmanifest, our bodies and minds allow us to realize our true nature as illimitable Nothingness. That is what the Buddha called Enlightenment.

There is no enlightenment to be found but in this very life, in this very body.

Nothingness does not threaten our humanity; in fact, it is the very ground that makes us fully human. Compassion, love, and kindness are all expressions of an intuitive understanding of our shared Non-being, the unmanifest Absolute that underlies all of existence.

Science has proven that we are all connected in beingness, but it takes the wisdom of a sage to penetrate into the deeper, more fundamental principle that supports even interconnectedness—the Nothingness that precedes 'being' altogether.

This is God, the great empty Nothingness of Non-being.

Awakening to Nothingness does not result in annihilation, but the exact opposite. Realizing that our lives spring from the rich, bountiful Void that is prior to 'being', we become reinfused with a vigor and vitality that we probably only experienced during intermittent moments of peak clarity and insight.

In that sense, Nothingness represents the ultimate affirmation. It does not dismiss or devalue existence; rather, it is a resounding, "Yes, yes, YES!" to life itself. For Nothingness is the mother of all 'being', the creative center from where imagination and inspiration flow. Our lives and all of existence are testimony to the fruitful plentitude that Nothingness provides.

There is no freedom like that of realizing Non-being, for the liberation it offers is not an escape from 'beingness', but a freedom *within* 'beingness.' A freedom to fully *be.* Awakening to Non-being transforms and redeems our lives and all of 'beingness' itself. It is the ultimate actualization of 'being.'

Luckily, we do not need to be a yogi, mystic, monastic, or hermit to discover our fundamental nature of Non-being. We experience Nothingness every night, for in our truest sense, we *are* Nothingness.

Awakening is the realization that not only can we never separate from Nothingness—for it is our true nature—but that there is no 'I' in the first place to be separate.

The sun, the stars, the earth, they are all manifestations of Nothingness. As are you and I. In truth, there is only Nothingness.

And that is God's true name.

Appendix I

Some readers may be wondering why I say that awareness is not the Absolute, despite the fact that so many ancient scriptures and eminent teachers say that they are identical. For instance, Nisargadatta taught that consciousness is rooted in (and therefore limited to) the physical human form, while awareness transcended the individual body and was actually the Absolute—that everything is Universal Consciousness.

This is more of an instructive approach than a philosophical commitment. If pressed as to whether the Absolute is awareness or not, I would say, like Huang Po did, that, "Mind is not mind, yet neither is it no-mind."

In Nothingness, there is some degree of awareness present—it is not how most people imagine brain death—albeit unconditioned, object- and subjectless. The Consciousness (for lack of a better word) of Non-being is so subtle that the moment we try to reflect upon it to check if we are conscious, we are jarred back into 'being' and into our ordinary dualistic consciousness. I hesitate even to call this experience "pure subjectivity," for that invites a metaphysical position that I am not willing to support.

In the end, to paraphrase Socrates, all that I know is Nothing.

This Consciousness has shed all of the characteristics that people normally identify with awareness, such as perspective, spatial and temporal contexts, objects, ownership, etc. Yet, if there were no awareness, then it would be impossible to differentiate the numinous Nothingness from how people conventionally conceive of blankness or being comatose.

Personally, I think that differentiating between Nothingness and consciousness is helpful, and that is my ultimate goal—to help people realize Non-being or Absolute Consciousness. At *that* point, I can care less whether people call it Nothingness, God, Brahman, Buddha Nature, One Mind, Universal Consciousness, or a kangaroo.

Names at *that* point, after the Absolute has been realized, are insignificant.

Appendix II

Verses

Vast Emptiness, Nothing Holy

God is Nothing.
Buddha is Nothing.
The world is Nothing.
You and I are Nothing.

In reality, there is only Nothing.

Nothingness is beyond any words or categories;
it defies all attempts to reduce it to a mental object or concept.

Nothingness cannot be perceived with any sense organ.
In order to realize Non-being, 'you' must cease being.

Reduce yourself to Nothingness by cutting through
the delusion that you ARE.

You are NOT. All that can be said is
"Nothing."

Not "Nothing exists,"
but simply "Nothing."

You are NOT:
you are not your eyes, ears, nose, tongue,
body, mind, emotions, senses, perceptions,
awareness, consciousness, memories, roles.
or anything imaginable.

If you can conceive of it, you are NOT that.

Negate all of these false identities and definitions of yourself.

You are none of them.

Abandon your attachment to them and dwell in Nothingness.

When all conceptual and perceptual categories

have been relinquished,
we lay the Absolute bare.

Then Nothingness unfolds as the one reality,
the world a mote of dust floating on
the infinite ocean of Non-being,
a flash of lightning in the great darkness.

You are NOT

Whatever you think you are, you are NOT.
Whatever you can conceive of, you are NOT.
Thoughts try to freeze what is NOT into something that supposedly IS,
but actually cannot be.

Forms appear to be solid but are really condensed Nothingness;
In reality, there is only Nothing.

Form is a mirage
Mind is an illusion
The self is an apparition
Suffering is a nightmare

Whatever we can perceive or conceive is NOT;
Nothingness is all that there is.

Subtract "is all that there is"
and we come closer to the truth.

Buddha awoke to Nothingness
and named it "Nirvana,"
which means "extinction."
Christ discovered the Void
and called it "Father" and
the "Kingdom of Heaven."
Nisargadatta called it "the Absolute."

Each of these masters realized Nothingness
so deeply that he could convey its purport
with only a glance.

Ramana Maharshi spoke of the Self, which
of course is nothing other than Nothingness.

Devoid of marks and characteristics, signs,
conditions, change, form, mind, time, duality, nonduality,
and even space,
Nothingness can never be known.

Nothingness does not exist, nor does it not exist.

It neither is nor isn't,
is neither something nor conventional nothing.

"Nothing Nothing,"[11] and that is all that can be said.

---

[11] This statement lacks a verb such as "is," for the latter suggest a state of being that is untenable regarding the Absolute.

THAT

Anything that can be known is an object of mind.
Seek the unknowable.
Anything that can be imagined is imaginary.
Seek that which defies imagination.

Nothingness can never be reduced to an object of perception.
If you seek the Truth, negate all that can be known, imagined,
perceived, or experienced.

The Absolute is atemporal, unborn, and utterly unknowable.
In order to realize it, you must transcend all phenomena
and all ordinary approaches.

Nothingness is the one thing not subject to time,
birth and death, or being experienced.
Ask with every ounce of will, "What is IT?"

Nothingness.

Not the nothing of ordinary folk,
but the Nothingness of the sages and Buddhas.

Absolute Nothingness beyond the opposites of
'something' and 'nothing', 'being' and 'non-being.'

It is the great Non-beingness that disqualifies all conditioned things.

Do not be fooled by mere words or the arguments
of the ignorant—Nothingness is not lacking or negative in any way.

"Nothing" is a verbal tool to lead the deluded from the pit of
suffering to the unconditioned womb of Absolute Non-being.

Nothingness is not nothing;
it is the groundless ground, the sourceless source.

There cannot be anything without Nothing.

Homage

Homage to the Great Nothing

without which the earth and stars and sun
would not exist.

Praise to the Magnificent Nothing,
the mother of all Buddhas and *jnanis*.

Though words are crude (some call
it Brahman, God, Tao, Buddha),
I call it Nothingness.

Markless, signless, unborn, unconditioned,
deathless. Beyond time or space. stains or purity,
Nothingness calls us all home.

It is our true name.
Dark, silent, still, void, and utterly unknowable,
Nothingness is the great womb from which we never leave.

Who can sing praise loud enough to honor
exalted Nothingness?
Whose knees can bow low enough,
hands write enough,
hearts open wide enough?

The best obeisance we can perform
is to look inwards and see for ourselves
the fertile Nothingness in our hearts—
prior to awareness, to our births, even to the dawn of the universe.
Allow ourselves to return to Nothing.

The greatest gift we can bestow is to recognize the Nothingness
in everything—the sky, grass, birds, music, and especially ourselves—
for there is only Nothingness.

May all beings awaken to the one true nature:

Praise Nothingness,
return to Nothingness,
for ultimately you, God, and all beings
are Nothingness.

Works Cited

The Zen Teachings of Huang Po edited by John Blofeld

In Praise of Nothing: An Exploration of Daoist Fundamental Ontology by Ellen Marie Chen

Consciousness and the Absolute: The Final Talks of Sri Nisargadatta Maharaj edited by Jean Dunn

Tao Te Ching translated by Gia-Fu Feng

"Nothing is Sacred" by Alan Gullette

Sitting in Oblivion: The Heart of Daoist Meditation by Livia Kohn

"Ayin: The Concept of Nothingness in Jewish Mysticism" by Daniel C. Matt

Dropping Ashes on the Buddha edited by Stephen Mitchell

The Principal Upanishads translated and edited by Swami Nikhilananda

The Teachings of Ramana Maharshi edited by Arthur Osborne

Macbeth by William Shakespeare

The Zen Doctrine of No-Mind by D.T. Suzuki

The Courage to Be by Paul Tillich

The Complete Works of Chuang Tzu translated by Burton Watson

Ask the Awakened by Wei Wu Wei

About the Author

Andre Doshim Halaw is a Zen Buddhist monk in the Five Mountain Zen Order. He is also the guiding teacher of the Original Mind Zen Sangha in Princeton, NJ. In November 2012, Andre received *inka* (independent teaching authorization) from his teacher, Zen Master Wonji Dharma (Paul Lynch).

Andre writes two blogs, www.originalmindzen.blogspot.com, and www.absolutenothingness.wordpress.com. He is the author of five books: *Neti-Neti Meditation, Brand-Name Zen, The Heart Sutra, God is Nothingness,* and *No-Mind.* He also writes the occasional novel.

If you enjoyed reading this book, please consider leaving a review on Amazon or wherever you purchased it.

.